Scop

Helen Shay

Nettle Books

Scop by Helen Shay

Published by Nettle Books
www.nettlebooks.weebly.com

Classification: Poetry
ISBN: 978-0-9933729-2-6

Helen Shay has asserted her right under the Copyright, Designs and Patents Act 1988 to be identified as the author of this work.

Opinions expressed are not necessarily those of the author, editors or publishers.

© 2017. Copyright of the poems remains with the author. All rights reserved.

Front cover design: Dan Shay

Contents

Storyteller	9
Heavy Metal	10
Dust to… `	11
Making Hot Chocolate for Wendy Cope	12
Footsteps	13
Letting Go	14
Brolly	15
Tea with Auntie Olive	16
The Golightly Guide to Earrings	18
Sex (Three-lettered Enigma)	19
Scop	20
O Tell Me the Lie About Love	23
Happy Ever After?	24
The Tide Turning	25
Faultless Design	26
Distillers of Death	27
Shades of Grey	28
Ice Maiden	30
Late August	31
Gagging for It	32
Siren Song	33
Nursing Change	34
Fungus Fetish	35

Orpheus in the Underground	36
Mothers and Daughters	38
Three Haiku	39
Discrimination	40
Ode to the Egg	41
Lifting the Veil	42
All for Love?	44
Source	47
The New Ophelia	48
GRIPING	49
What George Orwell Would Say	50
Three Unspoken Words	51
To Her Daughter on Going to the Bath	52
Thin Line	52
Heartbreak	53
Femme Fatale	54
Love Song	55
The F-Word	56
Puzzle	58
Don't Mention the Scottish Play	59
Lullaby	59
Rest in Peace David Bowie	60
Shredded Letters	61
By Halves	61

Leaving the Land Baby	62
Shakespeare Through the Looking Glass	63
A Rainy Day Woman's Half and Half Rap	64
Queen Harriet	66
Painfully Shy	68
The Wisewoman	70
Limerick for Harrogate	71
Hello Yellow Brick Road	72
Spuds	73
The Vampyre of Skegness	74
Providence	76
White Collar Wrapper	77
The Huntress	78
It's in the Genes	79
Flat 3, 6 Royal Crescent	80
Walk of Shame	83
Death By…?	84
Hawking	86
The Perfect Time Machine	88
Only Words	89

What other poets say about Helen Shay

Helen Shay is a writer with staying power. She's worked away over the years to hone her poetry and her stage plays. She is unfailingly generous in her support of other writers.
 This collection reflects her growth as a poet – technically, metaphorically and literally. I've always admired the way Shay tackles such an incredibly wide set of subjects with her poetry and her plays.
 Enjoy her breadth of field on the world, her use of language, and her great sense of humour.
Char March

Helen Shay is an enthusiastic and dynamic poet and a supportive and encouraging facilitator of others' work.
Gill Lambert

A linchpin of the Yorkshire spoken word scene. As compere and performer, Shay's enthusiasm for poetry and prose is matched only by her exuberant performances – she puts her mind, soul and body into her all her work. And she is all woman!
Mark Connors

A passionate and powerful poetic writer, Helen describes a world rich in the senses, with language eager to encapsulate and inspire.
Matt Nicholson

Poetry was always 'the fun stuff'

Alongside writing drama and other fiction/non-fiction, completing an MA, delivering workshops and holding down a legal career – not to mention dealing with that crazy little thing called life – there has always been dabbles of poetry.

More recently I took over running a monthly poetry event (*Poems, Prose & Pints*, Harrogate), which brought me much more into the 'scene' – that teeming womb of talent that currently exists amongst Yorkshire poets. I was also elected on the Society of Authors' Prose & Spoken Word committee, helping to improve terms for poets. Suddenly it seemed to get more serious.

Scop arose from this. It is an Old English word for a *poet* and with temerity I claim it for this collection. The title poem was originally written for and performed at Glastonbury Poets Tent (amidst some very mud-coated fun!) when I was lucky enough to be amongst guest poets, asked to write on an anti-slavery theme.

Feeling my northern voice might seem false amongst such as obvious American south subjects, I turned inwards to my own Anglo-Saxon culture, all too often intertwined in such wrongs. Shamelessly I have 'stolen' the odd line from certain Old English verse, hoping indirectly to connect with those wonderful, resonant *scops* of an earlier era and hoping to come under the same umbrella.

Whilst it may now be a larger part of my writing life, poetry still can't help but remain 'fun stuff'. I hope that any reader of this collection will find something to think about, but also ultimately to enjoy!

Helen Shay

This book is dedicated to family and friends,
who have been so supportive,
together with the creatively-encouraging
Yorkshire poetry/spoken word scene in
general, especially those enthusiastic
performers/attendees who come along to
Poems, Prose and Pints at the Tap & Spile,
Harrogate – with also HUGE thanks to the
landlord and staff there!

Storyteller
(published in *Binary Star*)

If I could Scheherazade
my way into you; through
each line, web and weave
inside your mind,
as you read,
along and
between.
If I could,
then....

If I could only symbolise,
moralise or allegorise
the meaning behind
the fantasy; each
slayed dragon, a
reason to shed
your armour.
If I could
then ....

If I could for just 1001 nights
lock you in my cave of words,
then genie you out and
Sinbad you over the sea,
roll you in a magic carpet
until you whisper,
'Open sesame'.
If I could
then....

...you'd come back again
and again and again ...

Heavy Metal

(published online by Leeds University as part of Helen Mort's *Leads to Leeds* Project, working with Bee Smith and performed 2 July 2016 in Poetry@theParsonage, Bronte Festival)

It never sang you to sleep, only
drummed into your dreams.
At seven years old, my lullaby
was iron clang swing of night-
shift down at Kirkstall Forge.

Seemed natural as the leaves
on Bramley Fall Wood trees.
Hammer soundscape to a stage
industrial-scaled. In its wings, we
kids played kick-can-and-hop-it.

The dark thud seemed eternal,
vortexing all into its domain,
beating out unseen shapes,
nurturing our West Leeds patch
with its nightly grand opera.

But there was no Wotan,
no ring of gold and I was no
Brunhilda. Just school dinners
and fish 'n' chips on Friday night.
So pass the eleven plus or else.

My father was an engineer not a god.
His world of crankshafts and creation
hung up a *no entry* sign for girls
(except for page three girls hidden
behind doors in his Works' locker room.)

But once I saw into the welding shed.
Glimpsed its sparking kiln of energy.
Metal seared, transformed by its magic,
teaching how flame, light and intensity
can fashion out anything you wish for.

Later the Forge closed forever.
Now it's just a station on the line.
Its metal music is over, out of time.
Yet I wonder how many of its children
go on, still dancing to it in their dreams.

Dust to ….

No more pills to pop
No more places to shop
No more lights to light
No more fights to fight
No more clothes to pack
No more tins to stack
No more money to buy
No more products to try
No more work or play
No more 'just another day'
No more sun as it goes out
No more scream and shout

No more golden lads and lasses who must
No more now as everything comes to dust

Scop by Helen Shay

Making Hot Chocolate for Wendy Cope
with apologies to Kingsley Amis' *Cocoa*

I bet it would be Cadbury's Highlights
or a mint-flavoured Options instead,
just to keep up with the Bridget Joneses.
'Less than 40 cals', the sachet said.

Cocoa or not, I'd make it good enough
for you and your lover, all the same
– smooth with bubbles on the top.
'A Horlicks by any other name ....?'

We'd slurp and talk about poetry,
sex, Christmas and the single life.
(Only I'm married – call it single
in parallel. Besides, I'm not much of a wife.)

You'd teach me things, through froth-choc lips.
(Yes, for a start, like how to rhyme.)
And how to fall in love, crossing bridges
instead of jumping off all the time.

And how to plead for copyright
without the legalese I generate.
How to suck eggs like a grandmother
– and how to be a woman and create,

which, inverted, was a favoured saying
of my grandmother. 'Now don't you create!'
mill-house Leeds, meaning, 'Don't show emotion'
or depart the seen-and-not-heard state.

It was served to little girls on Sundays

along with mash and mutton on a plate.
But we're big girls now (if dribbling hot chocolate),
future grannies who'll nag our girls: 'Create, Create!'

Footsteps

She does not walk
as I would have walked,
my creature, in whose steps
I would have followed
and now can only stalk.

She slurs and slips,
stumbles crooked in the dark
a blind bag-woman
feeling her way, mole-handed
towards some distant mark.

She hears the echo of my steps
but won't look back and see
what should have been
always remains here still,
ghost of she and me.

Letting Go
(published in *Leeds Guide* and *Algebra of Owls* anthology)

She doesn't cling anymore.
That sweaty, grimy, too-
young-to-have-a-wrist fist,
that clenched its red need
staining into my arm,
has loosened.

Instead, a cooler hand touches
mine. Still the dirt of play beneath
those nails, but each painted different
colours by her, experimenting
with bottles and jars.
(My bottles and jars).

Soon that hand will let go.
She'll have her own varnish
to silver each full-grown nail
with strokes, sluicing with sparkle.
Then she'll fleck her fingers out to dry
– like a wave goodbye.

Brolly

Left in your room.
Forgotten in that farewell.
But please keep it.
I can find another
and you may need it.
It holds the scent
of all my past rainfalls,
is guaranteed to give you
shelter from the storm.

It stands in blue folds
in the corner, its panes loose.
so slender-stemmed -
but once opened,
displaying its roundness,
becoming smooth
not a crease, every inch
of its skin stretched out
to protect and preserve you.

When you are under its canopy
it will shield, incubate you with
the sound of raindrops,
falling like tears of one
who can't be there.

Scop by Helen Shay

Tea with Auntie Olive

'Ninety next birthday, if God spares me.'
And I think you've got it right this year.
You've been saying it for the last five.
Maybe everything turns out to be right
If you just wait long enough.

It's only a matter of time too
(though minutes now, not years)
before you tell me once again
with the academic veracity
of an emeritus history professor,
of your days as a land girl.

I know those days as well as you;
so well, I wrote a play about them.
It was broadcast on the internet.
I tried to explain, get you to listen.
But for you anything 'digi-whatsit'
is a step too far into the future,
even to hear of your own past.

Still I love these Friday afternoon visits
to a lined and stroppy, five foot widow,
'Ninety next birthday, if God spares you.'
But familiar dread soon gurgles in my gut.
Because you will do it. You will insist.
You will make me a cup of tea.

In a fifties kitchen that has always been vintage,
I flinch to watch you with the boiling water,
your shaking hands that 'must warm the pot'.
I would do it for you but we both know
that would be one up for Him, Mr D

Scop by Helen Shay

who sits grimly reaping at the table
behind you, jeering at every spilt drop.

But today is a good day. No scalds.
Milk in the cup, then you'll be 'Mum'.
I remember your fingers before the lumps,
making me butterfly buns, scooping the cream.

Today, decades on, you make tea
without cake. Just tea. Nearly.
I sip the cup of whitened water.
Knew you'd forget the teabag.
Your smile says, 'Look, I can still do it!'
Cheers, Auntie Olive! Our ceremonies
have – despite all – been honoured.

I know when I leave, you'll forget
after five minutes, will wonder why
there are two cups on the sinkboard.

Is that how it always ends?
Here for a brief time, nothing
remembered except dregs
of what we consumed.

I think instead of consummation
not consumption. Something
changes, something transforms
whilst we're here and 'can still do it'.
What is shared will always stay.

The Golightly Guide to Earrings
(originally published in *The Journal*, Cumbria)

It was Holly herself, who said
you could tell what a man thought
of a girl by the earrings he gave.

So choose wisely. It follows
that the fate of every date
depends on the danglers.

The man who gives me pearls
gets me in artistic pose,
a coy but smiling enigma.

The man who gives me diamonds
will make me his best friend,
brightly sparkling on his arm.

The man who gives me crystal
gets me catching the light,
charismatic and candescent.

The man who gives me black
Whitby jet, gets me Gothic,
voluptuously vamp in velvet.

The man who gives me
Bette Lynch toilets,
I'll quickly flush away!

But the man who gives me
breakfast at Tiffany's
always gets supper in bed.

Sex (Three-lettered enigma)
(published in *Worldwide Writers* anthology)

Sex – a cover word to sell magazines
Sex – a language of sensuous braille

Sex – a woman's substitute for chocolate
Sex – a man's substitute for war

Sex – a union of sensation, more lonely than death
Sex – a tantric buddhist's path of enlightenment

Sex – one means of reproduction
Sex – top hobby, after DIY

Sex – the body's fight to renew itself
Sex – the orgasm's fight to exist

Sex – blue-eyed, pale-skinned and honey-mouthed
Sex – brown-eyed, sun-tanned and pouting

Sex – momentous and momentary
Sex – effervescent and eternal

Sex – light and loud, fun and frivolous
Sex – dark and dangerous, scarlet and black

Sex – fascination-full friend of endless descriptions
Sex – chimeric-silencer of unanswered questions

        Sex – the Betrayer
        Sex – the Life-giver

Scop

(originally written for Glastonbury Poet's Tent when abolition of slavery was that year's theme set for guest poets)

Veni, vidi, vici!
Forget the Latin
they taught you at school.
I'll put it in plain Anglo-Saxon,
seeing as that is what I am.
A plain Anglo-Saxon, who
came, saw and conquered.
'I invaded, I took, I enslaved'.

Yes, we came here, a few years back,
Angles and Saxons, and the odd Jute.
Seafarers seeking these stormy, soggy isles.
Hreosan hrim and *snaw haegle gemenged*
And now it's ours – our Angle-land.
Invaded, taken and enslaved.

After all, we weren't the first.
There was old Julius for a start.
He was a Caesar after my own heart.
A chieftain like me, a leader, a thane
amongst the warriors. My role model,
just as Alexander was before for him.
Veni, vidi, vici!
Invade, take and enslave.

Strange to think that a pope
should see our bright hair and
pink-fresh flesh as angel-like.
They should ask the Celts
how angelic we have been.

Scop by Helen Shay

We overthrew their chieftain,
their once and future king,
with his round table, where
all men were to be equal.
In your dreams, mate!
Invade, take and enslave.

Yet, tonight in the mead-hall,
my scop sang a strange song.
After tales of Beowulf and Grendel,
(and scary, scary Grendel's Mum!)
my own scop – chief amongst bards —
sang of a vision. I do not like it
when my scop has visions.
A poet with a vision is
a dangerous thing.

He sang of other seafarers
to come long after. Warriors
from across the sea, like us,
in swift ships, like dragons flying,
carrying thirsty swords to slash
through our shield walls, singing
songs of their Valhalla.
Invade, take and enslave.

Scop by Helen Shay

Worse still, the poet sang on
to tell how, in time after that,
some French bastard will
become Conquerer here,
and we ourselves the slaves.
Oh, *hwaer sindon seledreamas?*

It stayed in the scop's song.

Invade, take and enslave.
Veni, vidi, vici!

Echoing on and on,
down from my history
all the way into yours
until all are invaded,
taken and enslaved.

So when will it stop?
I asked the scop, but
his song faltered. First
free yourself, he said.
Make the tribes
promise....

I laughed. Promises
only live in songs.

Later I left the hall.
The ale tasted
sour tonight.

O Tell Me the Lie About Love
(with apologies to W H Auden)

Tell me it's wholesome as honey,
and fell for me at first sight.
Tell me it will love me forever,
and doesn't just think that it might.

Tell me it's tall, dark and Italian
and sings La Traviata on the phone.
Tell me it will love me forever,
and call me, when it gets home.

Tell me it's in it for the long-haul
and I can believe all that it says.
Tell me it will love me forever
(and in lots of innovative ways).

Don't tell me it's blind and fickle,
will never leave the single life.
Tell me it will love me forever,
and take only me to be its wife.

Tell me no truths.
Give me no proofs.
Tell me it will love me forever.
O tell me the lie about love.

Scop by Helen Shay

Happy Ever After?

If life were a fairy tale,
I'd rather be the witch.
Not some pretty princess.
But a mean, magical bitch!

I'd give every Prince Charming
a huge hug and soppy snog.
Then with one enchanted kiss,
turn him neatly into a frog.

I'd bake Hansel and Gretel
all in a gingerbread pie.
Lace Sleeping Beauty's spindle,
so she'd not sleep, just die.

I'd curfew all fairy godmothers
and make them stay at home.
Leave Cinders to ride on a pumpkin
and dance with the garden gnome.

Snow White would keep to her dwarves
washing seven pairs of socks each day.
Beauty would stay with her beast,
living the dolce vita, fun-feral way.

I'd wither away Jack's beanstalk,
shave Rapunzel's hair real good,
omelette the golden goose's eggs
and steal Little Red's best riding hood.

I'd barbeque the three little pigs
and hang out at the dragons' lair.

Befriend the big, bad wolf and do
anything and everything I dare.

So let's make life our fairy tale
and tell the story our own way,
Then good or bad, light or dark,
live wickedly ever after every day.

The Tide Turning

Walking alone but never lonely.
Salt-smell, gulls' shriek, soft sand.
Waves run along like playful puppies,
then drawing back. 'Can't catch me!'

And they are right. I cannot.
Yet they will come again for a while,
whishing at my feet, teasing at my toes,
before sucking back and out of reach.

Soon the sun clouds and the wind chills.
I keep walking, now on damp but firm sand.
I may reach the harbour just in time.
The sea will leave me but I shall rest at last.

Faultless Design
(a tribute to fabulous poet Julia Darling, which has featured in events in her memory at the Little Theatre, Newcastle)

Not an elegant way
to remember you,
perched on a railway
loo, and yet the image
comes every time,
every train and every toilet.

YOU MUST PRESS THE LOCK BUTTON.
The sign is still there,
as you are too in that jerk
of memory and humour
whilst the train chugs on
and I guard the door.

Sharing your poetically
surreal humiliation
has saved me from it
many times, more
than that overlooked
absurd notice.

Your sense of fun
has enlightened
my travel. It seems
that your poetry
keeps on pressing
my UNLOCK button.

I picture you
gazing helplessly…

above naked knees
a forever pure
poetry virgin,
smiling still.

Like flashes
through a tunnel,
such moments pierce
the dark of a journey,
sign-posted in the writing
you left behind.

Distillers of Death

T – oo little, too late.
H – arry Evans at least tried.
A – pologies are slippery creatures.
L – ove remains their main compensation.
I – t is cheaper to kill than maim, remains the legal adage.
D – eformity in black and white 60s footage offers shadowy reproach.
O – f all those countless 'distilled' victims,
M – ost died within a year of birth,
I – ncluding her. Dearest and
D – ead, so loved and lost
E – ternally, my sister.

Shades of Grey

They wheel her in front of the mirror.
She wishes for an ordinary chair
like the other clients have,
but they have younger hair.

Blonde, brunette, red
and electric blue.
They have chairs.
Only her grey
comes on wheels
for the Thursday Special
offered to the Home.

Her face in the mirror grins,
as Jenna appears behind,
weaponed with scissors.
Jenna does not ask her if
she's 'going on holiday?'

A goldilocks toddler
wanders away from
her highlighted mother,
(fixed like a Christmas tree
in tin foil and bleach).
The girl watches the op
on the elderly patient.

It's rollers of course.
Always had rollers,
ever since the war.
Back in the 50s
her red curls rocked

Scop by Helen Shay

around the clock.
Waves of flames,
jiving and diving
through the night.
Now all that rolls
are the wheels
on her chair.

Snip, snip, snap.
Shampooed and set.
Her now thin, wire-wool
Locks are dismissed in
a final puff of lacquer.

Her face in the mirror
nods its gratitude
to the hairdresser.
Then the care-worker
pushes her away.

Laughter, as she leaves.
She turns her head
to see. Laughter
of the child, clutching
up to the light, and
laughing with delight,
at treasure scooped
from the floor.

Cradled by infant hands,
a glitter-ball of
silver hair.

Ice Maiden
(published in *Lamport Court* magazine, Manchester)

Out there, I soften,
play the golden girl,
smile for the camera.
Only here, I ice over
silver. Become all
they want to see.

My arse, for a start.
Short, pleaty skirt,
I hate. No more
schoolgirl dreams.
This oval arena
is my battleground.

Slip the thin blade,
slice, so I float.
Listen to the applause
that rises and falls
with each spin –
the weave of my spell.

Curve and swerve
across the rink,
a gliding flamingo
over the white glistening
of my element, wanting
never to – 'Stop!'

My time and turn is over.
I halt, arms high,
my legs, a triangle flag
of triumph. Then

back to the bench,
waiting, waiting....

Late August
(inspired by *Kitchen Diaries* by Nigel Slater, who missed out on the Icebreaker)

Miniature apples windfall
already in the garden.
Hard white flesh beneath
their blushing surface.

Even a few plums push
a slow portly way out,
to spread middle-aged
into autumn soon to be.

But I still pick the greengage,
clinging onto fruit salad days.
Whilst light remains in the night,
I refuse to let the summer go.

Gagging For It

I like to sleep around
when I read and write.
Have a tumble in the hay
with a poem, then next day,
a quickie with a short story.

In the aftermath I'll throw
myself at a novel (usually miss),
submit a sonnet sealed with a kiss,
flirt with film, then make
a dramatic leap into a play.

I'll stay up all night
with a fantasy – make it
a three-some (if it's a trilogy).
My literary nymphomania
is INSATIABLE.

I will suck on a sextet,
orgasm with imagery
(even tanka with a haiku).
Words – oh, yes, yes, yes!
Right words make whores of us all.

Siren Song
(published in online zine)

Years I've had of highlights and straighteners, counselling with curlers and of course 'How's your holidays?' Living for tips. Not that they give much. Except for that one customer: Miss Miranda Waters. She gives me pearls.
Arrives every Tuesday in a wheelchair covered with a blanket from waist down, though her hidden feet twitch weirdly beneath it. And that perfume she wears always smells fishy to me. She likes to sing while I comb her long hair, her voice rising and falling like the tide, telling of a far-off place where there are no demi-waves, just waves that are wild and foam-crested.
Miranda whispers to me: 'Sandy, come live with me and my sisters. Be our personal coiffeuse. We live by the sea where you can be free.'
I know she's mad and not really a mermaid. The pearls can never be real. But who wants 'real' when reality's like mine. Next Tuesday I shall answer her call and say yes.

Nursing Change

In childhood, India meant gifts
– Kashmir shawls from Uncle Edgar
in the Raj, whispered to have gone
native... taken a bibi, who perhaps
did not need shawls in the heat.

On the Western front, it was always cold.
She pitied those dark men, shipped across
in the name of Empire. Many now lay
shivering and wounded on the hospital ward.
Not enough bandages to keep them warm.

'Your eyes are strange,' he told her.
and so they must be to him,
pale-grey like the Belgian sky.
His were darkly soft, smiling.
East meeting West in battle mire.

He wore no turban like the others,
hair long, no beard. He spoke of
gods and the spirit in all things,
whilst she offered potato soup,
lumpy and lukewarm.

The anaesthetic ran out early,
as more casualties piled in.
Only garlic remained. But
he had to refuse that, never
saying just which god it offended.
The sun shone on the day he died.
She moved his bed so he drank the rays,

Scop by Helen Shay

whilst she fixed on the beauty of his face.

She vowed when the killing was over,
she would forever cast off the shawl.

Fungus Fetish

Love is like a cluster of mushrooms
– only could they be toadstools?
Some are red, and clearly poisonous.
Oh, but such a Snow White apple red!
Don't you still want to bite and taste?

And then others might even be magic.
What a trip they might take you on!
Or, like Alice, make you grow or shrink
but you will, of course, always change.
Yet to find the wholesome, the meant-
to-eat is never a task for the uninitiated.

What an art it is to find a good mushroom.

Orpheus in the Underground
(published by *Poet* and *Geek*)

Orpheus

I never look back now,
only down, as I play.
At my feet lies spare
change in a black cap.

Once I did look back.
There it was – the girl,
the home, the future.
Then it vanished. There
are many like me down
here, homeless but
living, only in music.

Eurydice

The descent is always the safer way.
Rimmed metal escalating into smooth
exit. Away you go, through the motion.
Life-in-death, death- in-life.
I wanted more. Not a semi-
detached marriage to a Ziggy-
wannabee, who thought, 'Boy,
could he play guitar'. (He couldn't.)
Was that to be all? So I danced.
Charmed the serpent, gliding
under my feet, rattling like
a bottle of pills until empty.

'Bite me,' I said and swallowed.

Rush of venom, freezing out
cold in my veins. My blood
at last feeling a flame. But
then I woke, still tied here
by a hospital tube.

Back with the nine to five
in pin-striped mini-skirt.
Dark commute where all
are strangers on a train,
swapping lives and deaths.
Flashing through tunnels
with no light at the end.
Emerging to throw coins,
– small change – to a busker.
Pennies for the dead. Close
your eyes. Pay the ferryman.
The price is fixed.

Hades

Hell used to be such
a peaceful place.
Then they shafted
the darkness with
their lines, their noise.
The gush of trains,
the clamp and suck
of stop and start.
Voices jostling
for air, vibrating,
jamming atonality.

An off-key busker
serenading a leggy
girl, who never looks
back. Why, this is hell,
nor am I out of it.
Surrounded now
by mortals, their
discontent, their
'relationships'.
Can't a devil
get any sleep
around here?
Not until the day
they look up,
not back.

Mothers and Daughters

Memories forged in the melt of love,
grafted onto us through toil and joy.

Fights against each other,
flights to save each other.

Moments past you were too young to remember,
moments future I may become too old to recall.

In the sharing our strength survives.

Three Haiku:

Spring
(2nd prize Waterstones Haiku Competition)

Planting daffodils,
back aches but belly flutters
with flowering child.

Never Look a Gift Horse ...

Harmless wooden toy.
Equine effigy, now safe
within Trojan walls.

Deviation

Roman road junction
turns from straight into dirt track,
jewelled with berries.

Discrimination

We
come
out from under
the cover. Raise
our arms against
each other's. Brown
against white. Positive
discrimination, revelling
in our inverted rampant
racism. 'Yours is better
than mine.' 'Yours is
more beautiful than
mine.' 'Yours is ... '
yours, as I am
yours. Yet
yours is
mine, as
we are
us.

Scop by Helen Shay

Ode to the Egg

So which came first,
Easter or the egg?
That's before you get
to any chicken. And
why ever a chicken?

Could easily be a snake.
It hatches too and gets
first mention in Genesis
before any chicken or
Easter or an egg.

Some say Easter comes
from dark Pagan origins.
Celtic goddess of chocolate
perhaps? Or something else
that came before chocolate?

But does anything come
before chocolate even
for a fertility goddess?
Unless of course the egg
and maybe that was chocolate.

'How do you eat yours, O Oestre?'
'In a candle-lit circle at midnight,
cream-dipped in the Green Man.'

Only nowadays they come in tinfoil
- hollow inside.

Lifting the Veil

And Leban had two daughters: the name of the elder was Leah, and the name of the younger was Rachel. Leah was tender eyed: but Rachel was beautiful and well favoured...
(Genesis 29:16-17)

They say every bride is
beautiful. But what if
she isn't? The bride, I mean.
Not that I'm beautiful either.

You'd have to look to
my younger shadow for that.
The one who should have been
here. I stand in her place
at the altar, a veiled sacrifice
to our father's bidding.

Makes you wonder who
is the biggest fool in this
– her, me or the stranger?
Though he's not so strange
as when he first came.
Then it was hate at first sight.
I smelt his arrogance beneath
the grime of his journey.

Then his talk of dreams and ladders.
I swore I'd not be a rung on his climb
to higher things. My father wouldn't
listen when I said I was happy

Scop by Helen Shay

alone. Making a career of being
an old maid, tending the livestock
(and my father, the old goat),
roaming the desert, as barren as I.

'We bait the hook with your pretty kid sister.
Get both off my hands,' he said, rubbing them.

So here I stand, seven years on,
seven years older and uglier.
Seven years labour to buy him
the wrong woman?

But now Jacob moves nearer as
ceremonial words float over us.

I think of the seven hot years of toil
that never dried his star-soaked dreams,
that slowly baked hate into love,
turned Leah, the too-cold,
the too-proud, the too-old
into this all too-willing
surrogate sham, searching
tender-eyed for a ladder into the sky.

I hear him beside me, hushing sighs.
His fingers shake, lifting the veil.

And I wait for his eyes to see
Rachel or, this time, me?

Scop by Helen Shay

All for Love?

That's the question I'm always asked
when they wheel me out for an interview.
But which love do you mean?
The Greeks gave it seven names.
No wonder, as goddess of them all,
scholars still see me as a 'dichotomy'.

(Excuse me talking with my mouth full.
Apples have always been a passion with me -
like roses, myrtles, doves, swans and sparrows
— not that I eat them all, you understand.)

You see, it comes back to origins.
Did I arise, sea-fresh and virginal,
coyly hiding (albeit naked) in my shell,
the sexless progeny of tossed
semen from some saturnine god?
Or was I just another lust-child of Zeus
and some easy nymph or other?
Aphrodite Urania or Pandemos?
Am I sacred or profane?

(Sorry, I'm slurping. You do at my age.
Juice of this fruit trickling down my chin.
They'll take me back soon, not that it's so bad
at The Olympus Care-Home for Retired Deities.
There's jelly on Thursdays. Maybe I'll let
Ares — my old friend 'with benefits', and
we're not talking incapacity —
lick the sticky off my creased breasts, or
have hubby Hephaestus give me a bath.)

Scop by Helen Shay

Perhaps, you'd better ask Paris, not me.

After all, he was the one to snub Hera's offer of
brittle power and Athena's cold dish of wisdom,
for that crazy little thing called lurve, leaving
his poor little wifey on Ida, lonely Oenone.

'Will the hottest woman in the world do you?'
I said. Instantly he gave it to me, 'to the fairest'.

(But I would really rather finish this snack,
if you don't mind, before my afternoon nap.
Talking and eating gives me indigestion,
not to mention sometimes flatulence.)

Did I arise, sea-fresh and virginal?
Oh, I've said that bit already.
Memory's not what it used to be.
You could ask my son instead.
Not Eros, that pesky boy with random arrows.
(It was more fun not to teach him to shoot straight.)
Try instead my human-child, Aeneas.
Through him, my destiny was fulfilled -
mother of Rome and western civilisation.
(That lad has made his old Mum proud.)

Now that's got you wondering, hasn't it?
Could that be the real reason I let Troy fall,
when I accepted the prize from Paris?
Did I have a deeper, fateful purpose
beyond kindling a cowherd's infatuation?

(Let me just have another quick nibble, then
I'll tell you. Only pass me another tissue.)

Scop by Helen Shay

You see, it was never any 'face
that launched a thousand ships'
or 'burnt the topless towers of Ilium'.
The cause of such ancient carnage
was firstly the flesh of this fruit,
its skin outshining even Helen's and
more satisfying than any lover's bed.
Oh, yes, yes, yes!

(Look, now you've got me giddy.
Sorry, what was the question again?
My mind wanders more than
Odysseus these days.)

Oh, yes, 'Was it all for love?'
Well, it could have been.
Or was it simply so that
I could be the only one
to eat a golden apple?

Watch the last bite now.
Crisp and sweet. Swallow it down.
Throw the core to the ground.
Leave it to chance – or fate –
whether the seeds take root,
whatever new strife it may yield.

(Now I really must go take my pills,
soak my teeth and have a rest
before bingo tonight.)

Meeting you was...loverly.
Hope you find your answer.

Source

Waves break
over stones,
desperate
to be
absorbed.

All lakes,
all rivers,
somewhere
are one -
source
and tributary,
as all tongues,
all words
become one
word.

Whenever
we meet
water,
true origin
of the species,
we meet
our maker.

Scop by Helen Shay

The New Ophelia

Lizzy Siddal, a shop assistant who became DG Rossetti's mistress and later wife, modelled – mainly in a bath of cold water – in 1851 for John Everett Millais' Ophelia (now in the Tate Gallery). She attempted to be an artist herself but died tragically (through a mixture of cold, illness, opium and possibly suicide) not long after sitting for this picture.

He wants me,
fading into the elements,
'garlanded fantastical',
sinking.

I've been stuck in this bath for days,
on loan to this 'artist',
who sees only the image
on his canvas.

Even at night, I don't dry out,
back in my own master's bed.
I'll be an old master myself one day.
Gallery-hung for a hundred years,
then on a thousand birthday cards
or tasteful notelets, left blank
inside, for your own message.

There I'll be microscoped, A5 enveloped,
still fading into those elements,
dying in time, to preserve in art,
a femme more fatale than
my real life merely fatal.

But look again, beyond
the gossamer dress and red hair

clawing at water that won't hold me up.
See me instead, as if emerging -
an unexpected Lady of the Lake.

Not 'Goodnight, sweet ladies',
coughing consumptive
from days in this tub.
Not model-wife and victim.
Reverse the image you see,
of the woman in the past.

Then, out of Pre-Raphaelite
divinely decadent bathwater,
look again. See me instead
rising.

GRIPING
(having a Cooper Clarke moment)

When you're stuck somewhere you don't want to be,
seminar, meeting, wedding or kiddie-winkies tea.
When you're tired and you want to go to bed.
But you're forbidden to go home instead.

When you write something and it turns out wrong.
When what's on your mind is some rubbish song.
When you love someone you just can't have.
When you've drunk too much and feel so bad.

When nothing makes sense and it's time to go.
But you get to the door and someone says 'No!'.
When like the Ancient Mariner, you're all alone.
That's when all you can do is moan, moan, MOAN!

Scop by Helen Shay

What George Orwell Would Say
(if resurrected today)

Well, bugger me!
Big Brother's on TV.
And so's Room 101.
Hell, what fun!

So just what happened to 1984?
Don't think I can take any more.
No totalitarian state? Shit, I got it wrong.
Good job then, I've been dead so long.

Instead '84 was Thatcher, shoulder pads and yuppies.
No communist take-over? What a turn up that is!
But with Room 101, can't you still smell a rat?
Your worst fears are today's news and that's that.

And as for Big Brother, is he still watching me?
You may not think so, but I could never agree,
with 'security' droning down on through CCT view.
Oh, come off it, you lot, Big Brother is still watching YOU!

Three Unspoken Words

It was over.
After black rows
and red sex.
I gulped down
the soon solitude
and said it.

'Don't tell me
what I feel',
he denied, pounding
with heavy fist
on the armchair
of humble inheritance.

In that blow
my life fell
under the hammer.
Offer and acceptance,
a concluded contract
of irrevocable union.

To her Daughter on Going to the Bath
(published in *Binary Star*)

Jerking, grabbing, falling,
a fight for filthy clothes.
Milk dripping globules
– or even worse –
Indiscriminately deposited.
Struggle with dress, socks, nappy,
Vest pulled overhead at last.
And there she sits,
nude and beautiful,
transformed into a water baby,
unashamed and radiant.

Thin Line
(published in *Writers Viewpoint*)

I hate you
for your voice,
deep and toe-curling;
for those `gods are jealous' looks ;
for blue eyes, dark and dilated;
for your hand on my waist,
clasping, clenching, claiming;
for being hers and mine
and who knows'?
But most of all
for knowing why
I hate you.

Heartbreak

Anaesthetist's needle chills
my father's body, as I shiver
alone in a waiting room.
Surgeon gloves himself up, ready
to repair the latest broken doll.

Hands move slowly, precisely
on the clock above me and,
I hope, in there. If I were to
push them back, would that
muscle beat back in time?

His hands would then be there
curing all, fixing crashed toys
to crashed teenage heart,
patchworking my life into
reluctant self-sufficiency.

But the clock moves on.
It is *my* hands that work,
writhing over how late it is,
wondering if he will be home.

It is *my* turn and time
to have the strength.
As the hands meet
and the hour comes,
the operation is over.

Scop by Helen Shay

Femme Fatale
(published in *How Am I Doing for Time*? PPP anthology)

It's a long time since I've been in an art gallery. They're not really for the likes of me. Musical hall is more my haunt, after a long week spinning and carding at the mill. But this exhibition's causing quite a stir in Manchester, so why shouldn't I come along too?

I could have been up there like those women. I modelled for a picture too once. You won't know that artist though. She was a woman and exhibited under her brother's name. But I was just as divinely decadent as this lot hanging in here. After all I've got those sought-after, fashionably pale, consumptive looks. It comes of working until you drop.

I was a fallen woman, just like those the Brotherhood loved. *The Mystic Circle* was the title of the picture in which I posed. I made as fatale a femme as those by Rossetti lined up here, from poor Lizzy Siddal to Janey Morris in so many guises. It's amazing how a Victorian middle-class Arts and Crafts housewife could lead a double life ranging from Syrian goddess to evil demoness. That's art for you, I suppose. Yet I can out-Lady-of-Shallot any of these here. I am more than my image. I am real.

Not that I'm against such images in themselves. Look at the colours – magenta, gold and sapphire – and those sensuous details, with even every blade of grass painted in pristine focus like in the latest daguerreotype. Then those opulent central figures. Woman as a fascination, woman as a muse, woman as an inspiration. I suppose there are worse things a girl can end up as. Take a trip round Moss Side, if you want to see that. But aren't we more than just pretty pictures? More than just inspiration to a few opium-soaked Bohemian-types?

I believe we are also the inspired. We too can create – or destroy.

Scop by Helen Shay

That's why I came here. To deface these very images I love so much. The only way I can make men see them differently is by trashing them. If only it had been the Pre-Raphaelite *sisterhood* instead.

The knife lies heavy in the folds of my skirt.
'Keep your arm straight as you slash,' they told me. Suffragettes are becoming expert in such matters these days.

So do I do it? All these beautiful fallen women with red-gold hair. I lift up the blade. My hand shakes.

Forgive me, sisters. This is for our grand-daughters.

Love Song

Because I saw
your face and I was a believer.
Because this
could be para, paradise.
Because never mind
I found someone like you....

Because every
pop lyric is now Song of Solomon.
Because every
corny phrase is suddenly Bible-true.

Does that
make my love a cliché?
How can my love
be a cliché, when there
is only one of you?

Scop by Helen Shay

The F-Word

The most over-used word
in the English language
is the most Anglo-Saxon
'Fuck!'

Only in London, they give it
the Southern phoneme.
'Oh, feck,' they say.
Still comes down to the same
over-used four-letter word.

They even put it on tee-shirts,
and then can't spell it.
'F-C-U-K'
I ask you? Who has a 'fcuk'?
(Some shag with the hiccups?)
No, if it's going to be 'fuck',
Then get it right.
F-U-K! Okay?

But then stop for a moment.
Ask yourself why the most
intimate of all human acts,
is the worst of expletives.

Get called 'a fucker!'
and nobody likes it, do we?

Scop by Helen Shay

(Being called it, not
the actual doing it.

Though some people don't
(like it that is) but then they
probably don't do it either.)

Yet, whether you do or you don't,
the word just won't go away.
'Fuck you!' it says,
when you tell it to 'F- off',
and there's no fucking
getting away from it.

Ah, well, maybe I don't give a ….
Still you know what they say.
If you can't beat 'em…

Oh, fuck!

Puzzle

If you were the jigsaw,
I'd be the picture on the box,
fragmenting, disintegrating
into dusty bits of cardboard,
between your fingers, laid
out to put into place.

If I were the jigsaw,
you'd be my last piece,
the 'ah, there' moment,
tapped into where you fit
in the whole big picture,
at last perfect and complete.

But the puzzle is never over and
it never turns out like on the box.

We stay as bits threaded together,
intersecting lines, snaking
and rivuleting through
the surface. Rounded
tabs slitted into half-
circle holes that
any moment can
be broken up
to start
again.

Scop by Helen Shay

Don't Mention the Scottish Play!

Too many hubbles, too many bubbles.
A cauldron full of toil and troubles.
Some true-life black and midnight hag
gave Macbeth its unspeakable tag.

Or so the proverbial old theatre legend goes,
as of course any genuine thespian knows.
Shakespeare inserted a real witch's spell,
forging words in Promethean fire from hell.

But I would rather have this dark 'unlucky' play
than all of Titania's flimsy flitting fairies any day.
Midsummer Night's Dream will not come back.
So I prefer Hallowe'en, and to take my magic black.

Lullaby
(written on North Island, New Zealand)

We sleep by the sea, listening
to the rhythm of those waves
stolen from our own evolution
going far back, past and passed
womb-beat of tide and moon,
surfing upon a half-heard echo
below the cobalt blue expanse,
a depth more than dark that
sweeps us into a different bed.

Rest in Peace, David Bowie

To sing a song of when I loved the Prettiest Star:

Everything but cold fire.
The warmth goes on
in your songs, your lines,
for we all moved up
to take a place
near you.

A Discipline
(a cut-up à la Bowie, based on extract of Russell Harty interview he gave)

Conceive something and
you make sure you are out
following through
in the morning.

That's a discipline of the house
whether or not conclusion
of your ability, you decide
and do it.

Shredded Letters

They stretch like fingers,
still trying to hold on.
White snippets, dappled
with broken-knuckle words.
Love in shreds.

By Halves
Published in *Algebra of Owls* anthology 2

I'd like, just for once,
to do things by halves.
The morning after,
quick peck goodbye.
A phone number
on the hand, washed
off in the rain.

A job not to die for,
A man not to live for,
no be all and end all.
Sleeping all night
as he boards a plane.

Just for once
doing things by halves
and feeling whole.

Scop by Helen Shay

Leaving the Land Baby
(published online as part of *100 Thousand Poets for Change*)

"No-one has a right to say that no water babies exist till they have seen no water babies existing, which is quite a different thing, mind, from not seeing water babies..." Charles Kingsley, *The Water-Babies: A Fairy Tale for a Land Baby.*

In the end it will happen to us all,
lapping at our feet, cleansing
away our carbon footprints,
chimney-sweep soot-prints
with oceans of dramatic irony.

It will swallow our smutty limbs
and lick over our stained bodies
until we surrender to its seduction,
float downstream to some new pool
of water that was once Greenland.

And we will each be washed clean
– whether a Tom, a Grimes or an Ellie –
drowned into what we all once were
in Earth's first womb. A water baby,
back in some primordial soup sea,
done-as-we-would-be-done-by.

Perhaps the strongest amongst us,
or simply those with luckiest genes,
will eventually re-evolve, reversing
Darwinian Lamarckism, into embryonic
fish state, breathing again through gills,
surviving silently below the surface.

And if in a fresh sea-bathed age to come
some humanoid-mermanoid creature
is at last to emerge, staggering ashore
on webbed feet as if some flat-footed
newborn Venus, able to breath again
when air is once more methane-free,
then let us hope that under water
he, she or it has osmosised the old
Victorian moral fable and shall
(Magdelene-like in penance)
always keep those feet clean.

Shakespeare Through the Looking Glass

To be or not to be,
that is the answer.
The question,
we forget.
Turn it around,
go backwards.
Be to not or be to?
But why not just be?
No 'to' about it, no
imperative purpose.
Could we just let go
the endless infinitive?
That is the question.

Scop by Helen Shay

A Rainy Day Woman's Half and Half Rap
(With huge apologies to Harry and Chris, Sunshine Kids who give a hundred per cent.)

'Mine's always half full,'
you say. 'Can't you see?'
But aren't you really saying
you've got more than me?
Measuring lives by the glass,
or on Facebook or reality TV.
Even your cute cat on U-tube
has got one over on me.

And what's in your glass
that's oh, so bubbeley?
Not plain old H20 but
Moet & Chandon surely?
While mine's meths on the rocks
washed down with gnat's pee.
Mug like that, who wouldn't feel
just a bit glass half-empty?

You think I'll run out of gas,
yet I keep going stubbornly,
thirsting on for more until
Fate serves me reluctantly.
Daring to order a full pint
but unable to pay in positivity,
you try bar me for 'Tut, tut!
Naughty, naughty negativity!'

You imprison yourself with
gurus' mantras incessantly.
Their self-help manuals help
themselves to your beer money.

Scop by Helen Shay

'I Can Make You Thin' and
everything you wannabee.
Give '7 Secrets of Rich Bastards'
for a positively reasonable fee.

'Feel the fear and do it anyway,'
is like a lemming's suicide spree.
Do you put your hand in the fire
because the flame's so pretty?
Emotions are there to guide,
keep you safe and find the key.
Hurt tells you when to say no,
not mangle yourself deliberately.

So let gurus dream their own clichés
because I don't buy it that easily.
Call it half empty or half full,
the glass has the fluid ounces I see.
Accept it for what it is and do
not be afraid to take on reality.
Think your own thoughts and
ditch the false mythology.

Make your own final choice
whatever your tipple may be.
Best bitter or just plain mild
or sweetest cider with Rosie.
Whether you brew your own,
shake or stir a Bond Martini,
don't live in mere perception.
Look to the light, take on lucidity.

Scop by Helen Shay

Queen Harriet

(Lady Harriet Sarah Mordaunt (1849-1906) had a dalliance with Edward VII, causing scandal in her divorce trial, during which her symptoms of mental illness were emphasised. It is debated whether these were all fake, but either way it led to her incarceration in an asylum for the rest of her life.)

This is my throne. I sit here a lot.
Sometimes strapped, mostly unstrapped.
They allow women freedom here.
Look, no bars at the window.
Perhaps it is my palace.

Chiswick palace, shall we say?
He can have Buckingham, my royal l...
Oh, no, not lover. Would I lie?
No, just my royal l-adies' man.
my close but lost friend.

I'm as withdrawn as the Queen herself,
but they dress me in white, not black.
I don't throw things any more.
Just a bad habit during the trial.
Lawyers said it would be 'helpful'.

Madness is not north by north-west.
Hamlet outside hides Ophelia inside.
As drama queen I got attention at least.
Here there are no 'attentions', wanted
or not. Now there are no more lovers.

Scop by Helen Shay

Perhaps madness has kept me alive.
It is respectable, even acceptable.
My family preferred lunacy to lust.
I have come to love my condition.

In this world, I am allowed to be me.

After all, Tuke is a humane doctor.
Here they do not tie us to wheels
like witches on ducking stools.
No spoons between our teeth,
should we get too 'emotional'.

This is my throne. I sit here a lot.
In the Realm of Puerperal Mania
I can reign as absolute monarch.
Sleeping beauty at last awoken,
I have no need of any prince.

Painfully Shy

One day I married you in the library.
Down the aisle between book shelves
from 'Constitutional' to 'Crime'.
But by the time I reached homicide
you'd walked out, leaving me jilted.

Next time was in the Family Law tutorial,
a group discussion on grounds for divorce.
Our eyes met and we were back at the altar.
But by the time my veil was lifted,
you'd gone. Desertion without cause.

I forgave you by the Contract seminar,
where we tied the knot in Las Vegas,
and honeymooned beneath a desert sun.
But by the time we made love in the Grand Canyon
you'd left. A chasm opened between us.

Throughout our dream married life,
all you ever said to me was:
'Is it Chapter Three for homework?'
But by the time I could say 'Errrr…'
you'd found an answer from another girl.

Fortunately in the Human Rights lecture,
I arranged her abduction by aliens,

Scop by Helen Shay

who ate her (very, very, slowly).
But by the time I got to your side
you ran off. 'Five-a-side for hall!'

A likely excuse, I thought,
consumed with conjugal jealousy
back in my single student room.
But by the time the party started,
you were there. Drunk with celebration.

Then came the dance. Your tugging
on my waist, hot and claiming,
the moves, the mouthed speech.
But by the time the music stopped,
whatever you asked, I could not reply.

So of course it couldn't last.
A secret one-way matrimony
based on blush and stammer.
But by the time I could look back
and laugh, I could only wonder.

Perhaps one day in the library,
outlawed, you too married me.

Scop by Helen Shay

The Wisewoman

In the listening dawn, she climbs
up to the Cure Garden, lying
on the slope below the shrine.

Clumps of dew-drizzled sage girdle
the path to 'Our Lady of the Crag'.
But she knows this place was
here before the Virgin's time,
senses its link to the old mother,
healing truce of maiden and crone.

She plucks the meadowsweet
to soothe her own swollen joints,
then harvests hawthorn that
always eases her failing heart.
Next she picks rue and rosemary,
ready for secret visits of village girls
who turn alone to her for help.
Then she stops at the thyme
just to savour its sweet scent.

* * *

Hounded by traffic and arthritis
she arrives into another Monday,
parks the car in St Mary's Street,
runs to the sign of the green cross,
opening up the shop just in time.

Masked in her white coat, she enters
sanctity of the pharmacist's realm,

her own knowledge stacked between
boxes of anti-inflammatories and
antacids, overlooking the lippy
and 'false lashes' mascara.

Customers queue for her wisdom
from cough syrups to condoms,
or seek discreet morning afters.
She, as always, still in her place
dispensing solace and assurance
alongside packets of painkillers.

Limerick for Harrogate
(published by Iron Press in *Limerick Nation Anthology* 2015)

A famous crime writer ran away to Harrogate
to escape cad of a husband and marital fate.
She has treatments at the Turkish Baths
But sulphur water was no bundle of laughs.
So Agatha went home to divorce and celebrate.

Hello, Yellow Brick Road

She put on the ruby slippers,
ready to click the heels.
But how do you 'click heels'
if you're knock-kneed
and the toes pinch?

Face it, they don't fit.
All that sparkling red
was meant for a witch,
someone with magic
at her feet.

Not a puppy-fat girl
in a blue pinafore.
Even if they'd fit, would
she want to return to black
and white Kansas life?

There's no place like home.
But what if home is no place?
Stay barefoot, walk bravely
passed the munchkins.
Hello, yellow-brick road!

Spuds

Treatises and documentaries endlessly
record Ted and Sylvia's eternal triangles.
One overriding moral to emerge – never
ask your husband's wannabee-mistress
to peel the potatoes. She'll only go
down the garden instead, enticing
him with dirty *pommes de terre*.

If only Mrs Hughes had tried,
'Sit down, sister, put yer feet up'.
Or a girly kitchen chat. 'Men!
Don't they do your 'ead in?'
But that wasn't Sylvia's style.
She threw down her marigolds
and thrust the knife at her rival,
declaring, 'You! Taties! Do!'
Cat-fight mash for the man,
who could tin-opener both
of them from a canned life.

And all the while, Ted stayed
out, picking the broad beans.

Scop by Helen Shay

The Vampyre of Skegness

Zlad, as everyone knew, was a bit of a lad.
Just like his great, great, great ancestor Vlad,
so they all said back in the Transylvanian pad,
away from the pitch-fork-waving village mad.

Lured by seaside tales of flesh, fortune and fame
Zlad set out in Drac's footsteps to make his name.
Setting sail to land in fair Whitby was his wicked aim,
so getting shipwrecked in Skeggie was such a shame.

One moonlit eve, he was washed up ashore,
coughing and spluttering 'I can't take anymore!'
From fang to toe, he was black, blue and sore,
and declared against this there should be a law.

But you can't keep a good blood-sucker down.
And so Zlad fearlessly decided to hit the town.
Above his shiny red-eyes, he'd wear no frown.
(Only wished he'd brought a change of gown.)

He got many stares amongst the local Doc-Martined folk.
Honestly, you'd think they'd never before seen a cloak.
And as the sun rose, he began annoyingly to smoke,
before finding any Victorian virgin bosom, in which to poke.

'This never happened to Count Dracula!' he bemoaned.
On getting his own juicy-Lucy, all his efforts were honed.
'Give me a Bite-Me-Quick hat,' he lustily groaned.
But a knotted handkerchief was the most he got loaned.

Scop by Helen Shay

Thirsting to feed, he headed towards a distant bright light.
It was Paula's Chippy, open every lunchtime and night.

But when Paula saw Zlad, it was love at first sight.

Against her big butties, few men could put up a fight.

So Zlad never made it to a ruined abbey on the coast.
He got a coffin in the flat above the fish shop, at most.
Yet for him, Paula kept their love-nest as warm as toast.
Small but cosy – give or take the odd bat and ghost.

He gave up vamping for Paula's salty slap and tickle,
with the odd fried Mars bar, curry sauce and pickle.
And to his buxom lady-love, Zlad would never prove fickle.
No longer blood and gore, but love-juices would trickle.

So they lived happily ever after by the sea,
having deck-chair love every night after tea.
Until one full moon Zlad said, 'Paula, marry me',
and from all vampire longings, at last he was free.

Providence
(published by Stairwell Books in their *More Exhibitionists* anthology)

You hardly see a sparrow any more.
Their sorrowful fall has been offstage
like Ophelia, and 'the rest is silence'.

In York, the geese have conquered.
Panto-dames strutting cartoon pride,
each convinced they lay golden eggs.

On campus they're cursed, as excrement
is spray-washed from paths pre-Open Day.
But none confront them or dare say 'Boo'.

Yet once I saw one die. Savaged by relentless
rush-hour drivers between the lanes, whilst
its forlorn mate screeched of grief in the wings.

The memory of that scream still sings through me
– the horror, the horror. Beautiful as any swan
in its tragedy, fateful as any life in love and pain.

White Collar Wrapper

This is my Ali-G poem, my boy-rapper what will be poem
The rhythms that don't come naturally to me poem.
My 'Everyone look, who's he?' get me on TV poem.
Yes, I know black guys do it better than me poem
But I can steal what I can see poem.
Then the girls might fancy me poem.
Get me some at last for free poem
Cos my left-hand is killing me poem.
Orderly queue now ladeeze and we'll see poem.
An heroic Hamlet to be or not to be poem.
Only that question is - is it real-ee a poem?
Of course I have my own culture
but I want to don a glossier milieu.
Forget all my real but boring history.
Beowulf and Anglo-Saxon geneology.
Boy-rapper is what I want to be
even though I'm nearly forty-three
with white, middle-class etymology.
Bopping with words physiologically
is always the best psychology
to sound cool and hide the real me.
Only is this really poet-ree?

The Huntress

Which ancient god or goddess would you rather be?
Diana the huntress was always the one for me.
Yes, she's the one who I'd choose to be.
Out in the forest and ever so free,
not like me.

In the woods all day with hounds at her knee,
not in an office or cleaning the lavatory.
Artemis of the hunt, all moonlit and silvery,
chaste and chasing whatever may be,
not like me.

For she's a goddess, not a wannabe.
Untamable and wild and 'can't catch me'.
In need of nothing and lets no-one see.
Tall and slim and oh, so deadly,
not like me.

But when she's sick of only ever hugging a tree,
the hounds are dog-tired and keep stopping to pee
and all she wants is a cake and a cup of tea,
perhaps then that perfect goddess could be
just like me.

It's in the Genes

The eternal battle
of nature v nurture
is long lost.

It's just there,
deep in the DNA,
the mad and bad.

Byronic heroes,
tortured creatives,
desperate depressives.

Nature roots out the unfit.
Yet these are seen as so 'fit',
desired as mates.

Blood line continues
even if they perish
by their chosen poison.

Those who survive are not
the Vincents or Virginias,
but those staying within reason

handing down batons
of creativity, hope of balance
against self-destruction.

Flat 3, 6 Royal Crescent
Whitby
31 October 2016

Mrs Elizabeth Eleanor Rossetti (nee Siddal)
14 Chatham Place
London E9
10th February 1862

Dear Lizzie

Forgive a stranger writing to you, but seeing you again today impelled me to do so. Across the century and a half that separates us, please excuse the lack of decorum this must seem to you. Only seeing you today, as I did, changed everything.

Of course, it is rather that I saw not you but Ophelia – or Millais' Ophelia as it is always spoken of – though to me it can never be other than *your* Ophelia.

My first viewing was as a young girl, about the same age as when you were 'discovered' by PRB. Sadly I was never the 'stunner' you were (though confess I tried dyeing my hair copper but it came out more punk pink than your languorous medieval look). I was studying DG's poetry (and must apologise for a temporary crush on your lover-turned-eventual-husband). After the modernists had condemned his circle as 'tinged with a certain pre-Raphaelite nastiness', my generation were rediscovering the passion, colour and intensity that you embodied for them. It seemed you were their art, even though they made your life imitate so much else.

Naturally I have seen you in all your forms; Viola, Sylvia, Queen of Hearts (by the way that title was claimed more recently by another woman who died young) and Dante's Beatrice in canvas after canvas up to the posthumous atonement in Beata Beatrix. I've even seen you as yourself – Miss Siddal standing next to an easel. That was the you I like best.

    Also I know of your very Victorian melodramatic associations. Disapproved of as a quintessential femme fatale, you first inspired that scandalous 'fleshly school of poetry'. Even in death you were not allowed to rest in peace, exhumed to retrieve his poems that bed-fellowed you in your coffin (when Rossetti needed them back for profit in this world).

    That grisly episode in Highgate cemetery then supposedly inspired Bram Stoker's staking of Lucy in Dracula. It doesn't get more Victorian melodrama than that!

    Yet, co-incidentally the actual young girl who gave inspiration for Lucy – a model for an image in print rather than on canvas – was staying alongside the Stoker family in the same building from where I now write to you, perhaps in this same room. She lived and breathed reality, like you and I, and now links us across time.

    Yet I tend to think of you in a modern light. A simple shop girl (in days when they were seen as 'no better than they ought to be', poor wages forcing many to offer other merchandise in the back storeroom). Maybe a precursor to Twiggy – ordinary girl becoming THE face. Arguably you were the first super-model. Then came demand to maintain the image, the pale looks, the slender form. The same pressure now makes anorexics of young girls and makes models live on coke. For you, it was laudanum. It was perhaps an 'accident' waiting to happen –whatever happened - that night of 10th February.

    Today you are remembered as the woman who posed for Ophelia. She too was no stranger to 'accident'. I think of you working with Millais, stuck in that bath so he could capture you fading into the elements and "garlanded fantastical". Then it must have seemed he was the master. Nowadays the painting of you is itself the old master, star of the gallery and endless exhibitions – not to mention thousands of special occasion cards or tasteful notelets 'left blank inside for your own message'.

There your Ophelia is microscoped and A5 enveloped in her gossamer-like dress that drags her down, red hair floating on the surface whilst she sings her descent to a Shakespearian watery grave.

How many times have I gazed at that picture? I have grown old over those years, whilst there you remain young and drowning forever. Yet today, on an impulsive visit to the Tate, I saw you in a fresh light. I recalled the Miss Siddal next to the easel. For you too were an artist, even if tragedy, social barriers, aspirational limitations, lost love, lost children – all too common in your age – intervened before talent could be realised. Perhaps in the time dividing us, some power has shifted. Artist no longer automatically equals male Romantic hero/anti-hero. (Tracey's bed was hardly that.) Women are at least more than mistress and muse, no longer corseted into conformity. There is a new Ophelia, who is neither used or shamed.

Today when I saw you, the image was suddenly reversed. It seemed you were not sinking after all, but rising from the water, bidding us, 'Goodnight, sweet ladies.' Instead you emerged. Lady of the Lake, no longer consumptively coughing in your divinely decadent Pre-Raphaelite bathwater. Today I looked again and saw you as rising.

So forgive a stranger, rushing home to write to you late at night, across time and worlds. But seeing you, as I did today, changed everything.

**Warm wishes
Helen**

Walk of Shame

Walking in old flat shoes now.
Leeds. Friday night. Late.
Street corners where I tottered
on stilettoes, still evoke
whiff of teenage vomit.

Shop doorways reminisce
of lost love and lust,
drains of lost heels,
toilets of lost weeping,
pubs of lost barley wine.

(As strong as a double-scotch
and half the price.)

I am no longer part
of bare-limbed hens
and tee-shirted cocks,
queuing at clubs.
The party is over.

Finally I reach the station.
Beneath the Paperchase
and Simply M & S veneer,
it remains the same. Only
I am on the journey out.

Scop by Helen Shay

Death by ....?

Everyone has a favourite death.
Not that you get much choice
in such matters, unless it's a pudding.
'Death by Chocolate' and such like,
and then only if they haven't
run out in the kitchen.

'Choose your poison,' people say,
but they don't really mean
hemlock or cyanide,
more 'G and T'
or 'a large whisky, please'.
If you answered
'belladonna on the rocks,'
they wouldn't get it for you.
'The barman doesn't know
how to mix that one,' they'd say.
And you wouldn't know either,
so you'd have the G and T.

So we all keep secret
our favourite death,
like an unwhispered
sexual fantasy,
some implausible,
untried position.

Though I have heard a
famous scientist confess his
– death that is, not sexual position
(though I suppose it could be both).
Can't remember his name, but
guess it was Roger Penrose.

Scop by Helen Shay

Any man who goes to court
because his topological break-through
ended up as a pattern on loo roll paper,
has to have a favourite death.

His was by black hole.
Now you don't see that
on many pub menus.
'Death by Black Hole,
served with custard or ice cream.'
(Mind you, some of the pubs
I've been in .....)

But Roger Penrose didn't want
custard or ice cream.
He wanted to elongate to infinity,
like a piece of spaghetti,
and just before his brains
turned to bolognese,
he'd find the secret
of the universe.
(Bet that would end up
on bog roll too.)

Mine's lightning – death, I mean
but maybe the other also.
Freud and all that.
Be nice and quick though,
and bright – in a Blackpool
illumination sort of way.

A look at last into
the eye of the storm.

Hawking

I am …
as afraid as you.
A great man once said
something a great woman poet wrote
'It is our light, not our darkness
that most frightens us.'
But what about that thing,
that other thing,
that lurks in neither light nor dark?
That thing behind you,
behind me, over there somewhere.
But now ahead,
waiting, always waiting
in the shadow half-light,
in the grey,
– hooded,
like a bird of prey.

Perched, waiting
like a bird of prey
– some great condor,
waiting for you
to keel over and
become its carrion.
Death – snake-long
and bald-necked,
evolved to slip and slither
in and through the carcass
– the ultimate vulture.

But let me tell you
about birds of prey
(me, who is as afraid as you)
not all perch and wait.
You can greet, accept,
– even love –
take off the hood,
bring it into the light,
train it to the fist.

Then it becomes a hawk
– your hawk –
whether lanner or kestrel,
osprey or eagle
loyal to you
in the hunt and the kill
absolute in its swoop
and in its grace.

Nothing more to fear,
until the hunt and the kill
are done. Then there is
no grey, only light.
and, like the soul,
the bird flies free.

The Perfect Time Machine

If I had a time machine,
I'd never make mistakes.
Hurt and humiliation,
outrage and cock-up
I'd erase with hindsight,
re-enact in a retake -
past made pluperfect.

I'd flip into the future
to hedge my bets
on equities, men and
the Grand National.
Then seize the day,
ditch the subjunctive,
living just for now.

But I have one tense,
and always the imperfect,
never complete, com-
pounded with participles,
pre-fixed with 'should',
'would' and if only 'could'…
find that damn time machine.

Scop by Helen Shay

Only Words

It's only words, when all's said and done.
Just a few lines strutting out to have some fun.
What's the odd couplet or two between friends,
when sooner or later, we know how it all ends?

I'm not a Hitchhiker's Guide Vogan guard out to exact a
                                               poetic toll,
though have heard poetry makes a great method of crowd
                                                  control.
Yes, it can make even Manchester United fans disperse,
when threatened with the prospect of ne-ver-ending-ver-se....

But I have only a limited amount of words
spouting forth like some queen of the nerds.
Words are all I have – not (as the song) to take your heart
                                                      away.
Yearning instead to give back a brief something for today.

A brief something that might help empower,
seed the words, make them grow and flower.
Bring us together to find some meaning
Whatever – in or out – our political leaning.

Something for now, this transient moment in time.
Maybe a handshake or a hug, caught up in a rhyme.
Words that are out only to communicate.
Words that perhaps you'll either love or hate.

Words that speak and can't much else do.
Words that are in the end 'only words' – for you.

Helen Shay...

Yorkshire-born poet Helen Shay has had work published in various publications and online. She has a Creative Writing MA from Manchester Met University (Distinction awarded) and was then tutored by poet Michael Schmidt of Carcanet Press.

Her joint collection *Binary Star,* with Irish-American poet Bee Smith, won an IL Convivio international prize.

Helen began performing with multi-ethnic group Voices of Women but now performs solo at spoken word venues such as festivals (including guesting at Glastonbury Poet's Tent – still has mud stains!), conferences and even a golf club.

She teaches creative writing with York University's CLL, and hosts Poems, Prose & Pints spoken word event every 3rd Wednesday of the month at Tap & Spile, Harrogate.

Also in Nettle Books

Poetry

Life Class
Michael Yates

A collection of more than 90 poems about life, love and plenty of other things that don't even alliterate! *"Delight in the careful observations and appreciate the wisdom of the depictions, for reading this book is truly a life class"* – John Irving Clarke in his introduction.
£9.95. ISBN 978-0-9561513-0-8

Non-Fiction

Flying with a Broken Wing
Sat Mehta

Sat was five years old when he and his family became refugees, caught up in the biggest migration in modern history at the time of Independence. His home was destroyed, his uncle murdered. Once very wealthy farmers, the Mehtas became destitute. Later, Sat suffered a broken arm – complications set in and amputation seemed inevitable. As he lay in hospital, a world famous surgeon, Professor Robert Roaf, strode on to the ward, choosing "hopeless cases" to help. Sat got a second chance.
£10. ISBN 978-0-9561513-2-2

Fiction

Pomfret
Edited by Brian Lewis

Ten stories about historical Yorkshire town Pontefract by Yorkshire writers including Colin Hollis, Howard Frost, Linda Jones, Robin Gledhill, Ann Rhodes, Walter Storey, John A Goodrich and Susan McCartney. Illustrated by Yorkshire artists including Jane Walsh, Barbara Smith and Dianne Ibbertson.
£8. ISBN: 978-0-9561513-8-4

Heaven Scent
John Winter

A comic novel set in the swinging sixties. Charlie wanted to be part of the sexual revolution but it sort of passed him by. But he and fellow reporters on a seaside weekly paper have something to take their minds off summers of love – when the sleepy resort is rocked by mystery explosions. Is it the Isle of Wight Republican Army?
£10. ISBN 978-0-9561513-6-0

www.ingramcontent.com/pod-product-compliance
Lightning Source LLC
Chambersburg PA
CBHW071314040426
42444CB00009B/2016